THE SCOTLAND STORY

AN ILLUSTRATED HISTORY OF SCOTLAND'S NATIONAL FOOTBALL TEAM

TOM DUTHIE

g

Lomond Books

A Grange Publication

© 1999

g Published by Grange Communications Ltd., Edinburgh.

Printed in the EU.

ISBN: 1-84204-005-7

Photographs supplied by D. C. Thomson & Co. Ltd.

CONTENTS

INTRODUCTION

It started on November 30, 1872, St Andrew's Day, when not just Scotland's but the world's first officially recognised international football match took place.

Fittingly it was in Glasgow, the city that would become the country's capital so far as football is concerned. The match was not, however, at one of the venues that have become synonymous with the game there, but at a cricket ground, Hamilton Crescent in Partick. There, on the stroke of two o'clock, a Scotland team comprising entirely of Queen's Park players met the auld enemy, England.

Whether or not anyone on the park or looking on from the crowd realised just what was starting, we can only guess.

What we do know is the countries who were to become football's biggest rivals fought out an easily forgettable goalless draw. There was, however, enough interest to attract a crowd of some 4000 to watch history being made. That convinced Queen's Park there could be a big future for the sport and they convened a meeting of the country's leading clubs to discuss what the way ahead should be. Out of that the Scottish Football Association was formed.

In all eight teams took part in that meeting and made what was to prove a momentous decision, though it is unlikely any realised just what a significant step they were taking. Present at the Dewar's Hotel in Glasgow were Queens Park, Clydesdale, Vale of Leven, Dumbreck, Third Lanark Volunteer Reserves, Eastern and Granville, while written support came from Kilmarnock.

In fact, the main item on the agenda was not international football but the organisation of a knockout cup competition similar to the new and successful FA Cup in England and it was agreed that a Scottish Challenge Cup should be held annually. To regulate it, the SFA was formed and while international football was initially no more than a side issue for the new association, its birth and the success of that meeting with the English ensured Scotland would have its own national team.

Since that first official fixture and the events that followed it, the relationship between Scots and their national football team has developed into a love affair. The ensuing 127 years of highs, lows, delight and despair have seen the population come to attach an importance to the team's successes and failures which defies logic.

This book will not even try to explain why that should be, but what it does hope to do is chronicle a wonderful sporting journey for a small but proud footballing nation.

CHAPTER ONE

In the beginning

It is no longer clear exactly whose idea it was to hold the first international, but an indisputable fact is that the birth of the Scottish national team, as well as that of England, took place in Glasgow on November 30, 1872. This historic occasion cannot be put down to a moment of inspiration from a single Scot or Englishman, but was the result of a chain of events that started south of the border some years earlier.

Football in the organised form we have come to know it, was born in England and grew quickly from the 1860s. When, however, the Football Association was formed in 1863 it was not the intention for membership to be exclusive to clubs south of the border and there is even some evidence to suggest "English" was left out of the title so as to prevent clubs from Scotland feeling they would not be welcome.

Scotland's biggest club, Queen's Park, were certainly wanted and participation in the first FA Cup early in 1872, five years after the Glasgow side's formation, would pave the way for a meeting with the auld enemy. Queen's were promised a bye to the semi-finals if they would enter the cup and although short of cash, travelled to London. There they earned a goalless draw with public school side Wanderers. Unfortunately the lack of finance meant the players had to head back north without completing the replay and Wanderers went on to the final by default. The Scots, however, had made a big impression with their fine semi-final display plus that willingness to travel so far and that added considerable weight to calls for a meeting of the two countries.

Leading them for some time had been the Football Association's founding secretary Charles W. Alcock. Perhaps more than any other single person, it was Alcock, also the founder of the FA Cup, who was responsible for transforming international football from dream to reality. In 1870 he sent a letter to the Glasgow Herald suggesting a meeting of England and Scotland.

While he awaited a positive response, he arranged four "internationals" in London. The Scotland teams for those games were selected by Alcock himself–even then finding Scots footballers down south seems to have been a relatively easy task. Well over a century on it is impossible to ascertain whether he showed any significant pro-England bias in putting together the "away" team and given his reputation for fair play that seems unlikely, but records do show the home side was victorious in the series. Either way, these games must have represented an important step towards real internationals being organised, but have never been regarded as genuine inter-country fixtures.

Such recognition for a game between the English and Scots would come only after an FA meeting, in October 1872. With Alcock present it was agreed that "In order to further the interests of the Association in Scotland", a representative team would be sent to Glasgow. In modern times it would take many months to complete preparations for a Scotland-England clash, but then it was all done in a few days. In fact, it could have happened even quicker and England were initially willing to play on Monday, November 24. That date, however, did not suit the Scots and the fixture was put back to the following Saturday, St Andrew's Day.

Queen's Park agreed to represent the home country and while this was genuinely Scotland versus England, there can be no hiding it was very much a Queen's production. As well as providing all the Scots players, the club arranged the venue, Hamilton Crescent in Partick. An initial sum of £10 was paid to usual occupants West of Scotland Cricket Club and when the takings at the gate reached the princely amount of £103, that fee was doubled. The referee and one of his linesmen were also Queen's Park men, but Alcock was to be an influential figure too, though not to the extent he originally intended. He was to have captained England that day but an injury meant his participation was restricted to running the other line.

The game itself is best described as an anti-climax, though a better than anticipated crowd of 4000 turned out to see the teams fail to produce a goal. England had expected to win, but the switch from Monday to Saturday meant many of their players had not enjoyed an ideal preparation, having had to travel to Scotland overnight instead of the day before as would have been the case if the game had gone ahead on the 24th. A poor match then, but the important point was that the ball had started rolling and Scotland's love affair with its national team had begun. He had waited longer than he would have liked for the first official Scotland-England game, but if Alcock wanted a return match, he quickly got his wish. It came the following March at the Oval in London and was to be the first of Scotland's frequent, and in the long-term often forlorn, pilgrimages to the capital. Again the English secretary was on duty on the line but before him were players from Royal Engineers, Wanderers and Clydesdale to break the Queen's Park stranglehold on the Scots team. Maybe that was not such a good thing because Scotland went down 4-2, though such defeats were to prove the exception rather than the rule in the early years of what immediately became an annual clash.

Football, of course, was increasing in popularity throughout Britain and within a relatively short space of time, it was booming. So much so, in fact, that by 1876 a meeting with Wales was arranged and our Celtic rivals easily despatched 4-0. Indeed at that time there was no disputing Scotland's status as top dogs. As well as regularly turning over the auld enemy, there would be 14 meetings with the Welsh before they could even muster a draw. Ireland, who arrived on the scene early in 1884, were also there for the taking and it was into the opening years of the 20th century, 1903 to be exact, before the men from the Emerald Isle recorded a victory.

This success in the 1870s and 1880s was a reflection of the strength of the country's clubs and while Queen's Park continued to provide the nucleus of the national side, the other successful clubs were well represented too. Certainly, no single player was regarded as indispensable and it was with an air of arrogance that the SFA would regularly rotate selection, confident in the knowledge that whatever team they fielded, it would probably prove too strong for the English and definitely outplay the Irish and Welsh.

One reason for these early successes could be traced to the fact that while in England football in its formative years tended to be a sport of the middle and upper classes, almost from its very beginnings north of the border, it had huge appeal to the working classes. Quite obviously that meant large numbers of Scots quickly developed an interest and clubs, particularly in the west, had a considerable reservoir of talent from which to draw players. So in turn did the national team and that was reflected in results like the 7-2 thrashing of England and 9-0 destruction of the Welsh in 1878.

By then the Scots had been smitten by football and as early as the end of the 1870s, just eight years after that first international, it was widely regarded as the number one sport in the land and the national team was being followed with the kind of passion rarely demonstrated in connection with sport.

CHAPTER TWO

Early dominance

England had come to Scotland in 1872 with the intention of helping spread the football gospel. As noble an act as that may have been, the Football Association would quickly come to realise their smaller neighbours were far more astute than they in understanding how the game should be played. That fact is clearly shown in the early results from the annual Scotland-England fixture. Between that first meeting and 1890, the Scots won eleven of nineteen clashes and lost just three. Observers of the time, on both sides of the border, were in general agreement that tactically the Scots were way ahead of their bigger neighbours.

Over the years to come Scotland would become renowned for a production line of players adept at dribbling and men like Hughie Gallacher, Alan Morton, Alex James and Jimmy Johnstone would become almost legendary figures. It was, however, the realisation of how effective a passing game could be that proved the key to success over those fledgling years of international fixtures.

The English approach, and to some extent that of Wales and Ireland, was simple. On gaining possession players would run forward until their progress was halted, at which point it would be up to their team mates to get on the ball and continue the attack in a similar fashion. In Scotland, the logic of players passing to a team mate before an opponent tackled them was quickly spotted and teams north of the border were encouraged to adopt this more measured and skilful approach. The English were slow to follow that lead and paid the price. Very often they fielded teams containing players of considerable physical strength, but frequently the Scots would run circles round them.

By the early 1890s, thanks mainly to the recruitment of Scots by English professional clubs, that situation was changing. Scotland could still claim to be the best of the four international nations but as the migration of talent continued, English clubs began to adopt the passing game and their national side started catching up. The Welsh and Irish improved too and by the end of the century they were no longer the pushovers of a few years before. That said, in most games Scotland were still beating them.

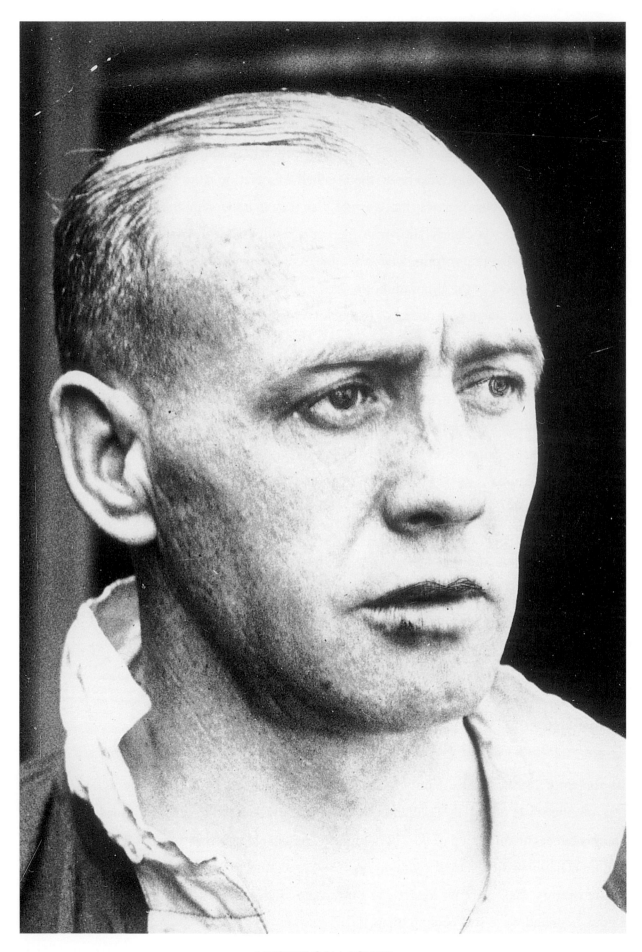

HUGHIE GALLACHER

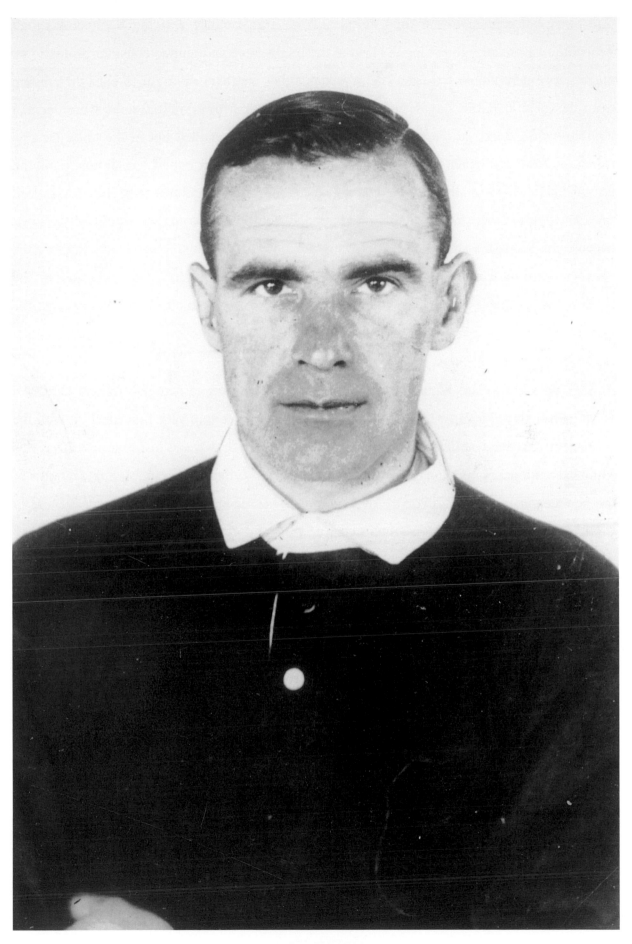

ALEX MORTON

The other big change in the final decade of the 19th century was the Scottish Football Association eventually following the lead of the English and agreeing to consider professional players for international fixtures. The acceptance that men had the right to earn their living from the game came in stages and for a spell only pros with domestic clubs were deemed eligible for Scotland, so the many English-based players remained out in the cold. Despite resistance from gentleman players who felt to receive payment for sport was almost immoral, England had recognised the pros eight years earlier, much to the annoyance of the SFA. Indeed for a brief period there was a danger internationals between the countries would be scrapped because the Scottish association did not want to expose its amateurs to such an evil. Once the home-based pros were allowed in, however, the SFA's position shifted quickly and by the dawning of the 20th century, paid players were the norm for both clubs and country and the days of dominance by amateur clubs such as Queen's Park were over.

As 1900 arrived Scotland remained well ahead when it came to international success. Of a total of 68 games played against England, Ireland and Wales since that very first meeting with the auld enemy 28 years earlier, forty-nine had been won, ten drawn and just nine lost. That was a quite sensational record and one which was immediately enhanced in the first few months of the new century with a 5-2 victory over Wales in Aberdeen, a 3-0 success over Ireland in Belfast and a 4-1 triumph against the English at Parkhead in Glasgow.

By now football's popularity among the masses was well established and that last game attracted an unprecedented 64,000 spectators. Of course that is a record that has since been broken at many grounds in many countries but the fact that it was sixteen times more people than watched the first international demonstrates just how the game's pulling power had increased. Meetings with Wales and Ireland were nothing like as appealing to the public, though they did regularly attract attendances in excess of 10,000 wherever they were played in Scotland–when the English travelled north one of the big Glasgow grounds was used, but the other games toured the provinces.

In the early 1900s football was no longer just a British sport. Scots, English and Irish were spreading the gospel the world over with, in particular the rest of Europe and South America proving eager disciples and on both continents the game quickly exploded. Given that, and the obvious public liking for watching the national team in action, it is somewhat strange to report that it would be 57 years after the first country-against-country clash before Scotland would be regularly fielding teams against opposition other than England, Ireland or Wales. There had been unofficial meetings with foreigners dating as far back as 1888 when a select side beat Canada 4-0 in Glasgow, but such matches were few and far between. In 1929, at the end of a decade of success in the Home International Championship, an inexperienced squad set off for the continent. Three games, against Norway, Germany and the Netherlands were played (the first and last were won and a strong German side held 1-1 in Berlin) and while they were also not afforded official international status, the trend of facing a variety of countries each season or so had been established.

The following year, 1930, saw the first official international abroad when Scotland beat France 2-0 in Paris thanks to a Hughie Gallacher double. As is explained elsewhere in this book, a lack of FIFA membership meant the early World Cups could not be entered, but a series of friendlies were played. These games were to show that the game to which the Scots had given so much, had been taken to new levels elsewhere and the early 1930s saw the team well beaten on its travels to Italy and Austria. Those reversals were on foreign soil and a 100% home record against anyone outside the other home countries was maintained until Austria won 1-0 at Hampden Park before 68,000 shocked fans in December 1950. That result represented a huge blow to national pride, though it is worth pointing out that this record may well have had more to do with the lack of games than the superiority of the team. The Austrian defeat was only the eighth time a European country had visited in the 20 years or so of friendlies with them. In fairness a large chunk of that period saw no games played because of the Second World War, the outbreak of which also marked the end of Scotland as a major footballing power.

CHAPTER THREE

World Cup Finals

Scotland, along with the other home countries and most major European associations, did not travel to the first World Cup in Uruguay and few on this side of the Atlantic seemed to care too much. Now, the best part of 70 years on from those opening finals, the country is as enthralled by the planet's biggest sporting event as any nation.

Indeed the World Cup, or perhaps more accurately qualification for the second stage of its finals, has arguably replaced the beating of England as Scotland's Holy Grail. Since 1974 in particular, when Willie Ormond led a talented but tactically naive team to the finals in West Germany for the first appearance on that stage for 16 years, at four yearly intervals the population has held its collective breath as attempts to get past the hurdle of the opening group have come and gone without success. Some of the failures have been heroic, some humiliating and all have been emotional roller coaster rides for what's come to be known as the Tartan Army.

Ironically, the best chance of making a real impact on the competition would probably have been in those inaugural finals back in 1930, a time when the national team was still a major power. As one of the two nations who introduced the world to the international game, Scotland might reasonably have been expected to take part. Two years earlier, however, all four home countries had resigned from FIFA following a row over 'broken time' payments to amateurs, so participation was not an option-a situation that remained for the finals of Italy and France in 1934 and 1938.

Qualification by right was achieved for Brazil in 1950, courtesy of a second place finish in the Home International Championship. FIFA had decided that was enough to earn a place, but in their wisdom the Scottish Football Association decided it would not be proper for mere runners-up to take part. It was, therefore, to be another four years before a Scots team would grace that stage. By then attitudes in Park Gardens had softened and qualification was also down to finishing second to England in the "domestic internationals".

Perhaps it would have been wiser to repeat the noble gesture of 1950, for Switzerland 1954 was to be a painful experience...

FIRST APPEARANCE–FIRST FAILURE

For the first time a team manager, Huddersfield Town boss Andy Beattie, was appointed, though picking the team was still the duty of a panel of selectors. In choosing a squad for the finals they decided to pacify Rangers' protests about being deprived of players for club duties and allow George Young, Willie Woodburn and Sammy Cox to head for the Canadian Rockies for a close-season tour instead of the Swiss Alps to represent their country.

Now such a decision would be unthinkable and even back then many other national associations put country firmly before club. While interest here in the World Cup was considerable, clubs still wielded enough power to get their own way. Nominally the SFA did have the power to insist players be made available, but having received a thinly veiled threat that the Ibrox club was prepared to challenge them on this issue, it was not a rule the association was confident of enforcing.

Whatever the rights and wrongs of the situation, there can be no doubt the influential Young in particular was badly missed.The giant defender would have been the natural team leader but it was not to be. In fairness talented, if inexperienced, players like future managers Tommy Docherty and Ormond as well as Neil Mochan did play and even had the missing Rangers and the likes of unfit centre-forward Laurie Reilly of Hibs been present, they would still have faced a stern test.

For the competition countries were placed in groups of four, though only drawn to play two of the other teams in their section. The top two would progress to the quarter-finals and to get there Beattie's team had to overcome the ageing, but still dangerous, Austrians and defending champions Uruguay, one of the few teams given any real chance of preventing pre-tournament favourites Hungary taking the cup behind the iron curtain.

As ever, when the Austrians were tackled in Zurich on June 16, expectation back home was high. However, while the players gave a good account of themselves–they were unlucky not to open the scoring early on–they went down to a single goal, scored by Erich Probst 13 minutes before the interval. That battling performance could not paper over the cracks of what was an unhappy group and the mood in the camp was not helped when the manager sensationally announced he would be quitting as soon as involvement in the competition had come to and end. That left an already badly-organised trip in danger of disintegrating into farce.

Beattie admitted there had been problems with SFA officials and it seemed the failure to allow him to pick the team was the main bone of contention. Preparations for the meeting with Uruguay, in Basle on June 19, were not good and what followed was one of the worst defeats ever suffered by a team in the dark blue jerseys. Those shirts, incidentally, were of the same heavy material Scots clubs wore during the winter months and on a blistering hot Swiss day far from ideal attire. That handed an early advantage to the more suitably dressed opposition.

As well as lightweight shirts, the Uruguayans had the benefit of being a class team. They were en route to an epic semi-final loss to eventual runners up Hungary and in their final group match showed their full power. They ran riot, hammering home seven goals to send Scotland crashing out of a competition, for which they had been ill-prepared and paid the price accordingly.

FOUR YEARS ON AND SCOTLAND STILL SEARCHING FOR A WIN

Since the formation of FIFA in 1904, Scotland and the other home nations have periodically faced calls to unite and form one Great Britain side. They have always been resisted but as thoughts turned towards the 1958 finals in Sweden, the Scots, English, Welsh and Northern Irish faced a different complaint. While it had been established all four had the right to their footballing independence, the use of the Home Internationals as a qualifying group was challenged, so for the first time the quartet had to face foreign opposition instead of each other as they attempted to get to the finals. If that was a ploy to keep them away from Sweden it was an abysmal failure because, for the first and only time to date, they all made it.

In Scotland's case doing that meant getting past difficult opposition in Switzerland and Spain. The Spanish were expected to go through and possibly even win the whole tournament but in the event lived up to their reputation as perennial under-achievers and the Scots topped the group.

As with four years earlier, the SFA decided a team manager would be a good idea and this time wisely moved to appoint the best man around–Manchester United's Matt Busby. Tragically the carnage of the Munich air disaster that decimated his fine young United team, would also deny him the chance to lead his country on the game's biggest stage. So, as Busby continued a slow and painful recovery in Manchester, the team set off for Scandinavia.

While, like 1954, the finalists were placed in groups of four, this time, more sensibly, they played all the teams in their group. Opposition was provided by Yugoslavia, Paraguay and France and a reasonable start was made when the talented Yugoslavs were held to a draw in Vasteras on June 8. Down very early on, a Jimmy Murray goal two minutes into the second half earned a confidence boosting point, the first in the World Cup finals.

So, just three days later, it was with a sense of growing optimism that the team ran out against Paraguay, but while Bobby Collins grabbed the honour of scoring the finals' 500th goal, the game was lost 3-2, with few arguing the result was anything but fair. That left a mountain to climb if the quarter-finals were to be reached, but all was not lost. If France could be beaten in the final game and Yugoslavia came out on top against Paraguay, the job would be done. Even a draw for the Yugoslavians would provide Scotland a route via a play-off against Paraguay. Of course, events in the other game would only matter if victory was secured.

That was the stumbling block and although a 2-1 defeat at the hands of a very good French team, including a goal from record World Cup scorer Just Fontaine, was no disgrace, elimination was a bitter pill to swallow for a nation that had again had high hopes for its international team.

GLORIOUS FAILURE

By the time Scotland returned to the finals, in West Germany in 1974, the event had grown almost beyond all recognition from what had last been tasted in Sweden 16 years earlier. Thanks largely to blanket coverage in this country of England's home triumph of 1966 and world-wide live television pictures of the near perfect Brazilians' third trophy win in Mexico four years later, the finals had become the most-watched sporting event on earth.

As they hopped over the North Sea, Ormond's boys were very much the underdogs, having been drawn to face the defending champions, then Yugoslavia again and, first off, the unknown Africans of Zaire. At least by now the old selection system was long gone and a full-time manager, Willie Ormond, had the opportunity to pick his own team. While his players may have lacked any experience at this level, the quietly spoken former St Johnstone boss had been in Switzerland 20 years earlier and had some kind of idea of what to expect.

With the team likely to be nervous early in the opening match, that the opposition was unfancied Zaire seemed a bonus. Based on what little information could be gathered, it was believed they would pose few problems. So it proved and goals from hotshot Peter Lorimer and Joe Jordan, the young striker whose dramatic header against Czechoslovakia had secured qualification, had the game won by the break. In the second half chances to win by a bigger margin were squandered, though given a second half revival by Zaire, the score seemed acceptable. Back home and among the 7000 Scots who occupied the terracing in the Westfalen Stadium in Dortmund, the result was greeted with tremendous joy. After all, it had taken 20 years for this win to come and the team were top of a group that included the world champions!

Cruelly, that failure to hit the target more frequently in the first game was to cost the team sporting immortality back home.

So too did the matter of a few inches in the Waldstadion in Frankfurt on June 18. On that night Scotland rocked three-times champs Brazil to the soles of their boots and came within a whisker of sending them back home in disgrace.

It has to be conceded this Brazilian side was an ugly imitation of the one that had taken the

WILLIE ORMOND

beautiful game to a different level four years previously. Mario Zagallo's class of '74 was more physical and cynical but still boasted world class performers like Mexico's goal-a-game man Jairzinho and Rivelino, the creative midfielder with a sizzling left-foot shot. Their presence did not seem to worry Scotland and with skipper Billy Bremner an inspiration, the players set about bringing their more famous opponents down a peg or two with a brave display that possibly merited more than just a share of the spoils. It was to be Bremner himself who came closest to turning a creditable draw into a heroic victory.

It was a moment those who witnessed it will never forget. Twenty minutes remained as Lorimer sent over a corner, Jordan headed it on to Bremner and his close-range effort slipped agonisingly wide by less than the thickness of the post. It was a classic case of what might have been, but still a fine result for a team supposed to be doing little more than making up the numbers. The draw also left Ormond's team with a reasonable chance of making the second stage, though to get there Yugoslavia had to be overcome.

The Yugoslavs had drawn their opening game with Brazil, then hammered nine past Zaire – controversial given that the Africans' coach Blagoje Vidinic was from the Balkans–and knew another draw would leave them ahead of Scotland, at least, on goal difference. It was a tense game but the tartan army's hopes were still alive as it moved into the last ten minutes still goalless. Then, disaster struck. Substitute Stanislav Karasi headed the opener on 81 minutes and qualification hopes looked dead and buried. In wonderful never-say-die fashion Joe Jordan equalised with just two minutes left to raise some hope, but as the players trooped off the field after the final whistle, news came through Brazil had beaten Zaire 3-0 and Scotland were eliminated by a single goal.

So that failure to score more in the first game had, after all, come back to haunt the team but that did not prevent players and officials leaving West Germany with heads held high, the only unbeaten nation in the finals and knowing they had proved they could play a bit.

CRY FOR US ARGENTINA

If elimination in 1974 represented noble failure, four years later it ranked as most embarrassing. Under the charismatic leadership of manager Ally MacLeod, the team went to Argentina not just confident about making the second stage for the first time, but genuinely believing the World Cup could be returning to Hampden. Decades later, that there was ever such a notion seems ridiculous and quite simply it was. For a start, no European side had ever lifted the cup in South America and even world powers like defending champions West Germany and the outstanding Dutch were wary of predicting success in the intimidating atmosphere of Buenos Aires. Scotland had a good team and were easily the best of the four home nations-for the second finals running they were the only British representatives - but at best they were the dark horses of the event.

With his infectious optimism MacLeod, fresh from a successful first year as national team boss, did not see things that way. He soon had the country believing his was a team on the verge of history.

Such confidence was boosted by a draw that placed Scotland with the mighty Dutch, but handed him games against "ageing" Peru and minnows Iran first. The nation believed that by the Holland game a place in the second stage would already be secured. Such predictions looked fairly sound when, after just 14 minutes of the clash with the Peruvians, Joe Jordan pounced to grab his third finals goal. The lead was a fair reflection of the early play but as Peru settled into their rhythm, the outcome began to look less certain than the manager had told everyone it would be before a ball was even kicked. Just before half-time Cesar Cueto struck to level the scores and it was all downhill from there. A second half double from the skilful Teofilo Cubillas provided a win that was no less than the South Americans deserved.

Unless you were Scottish, there was obvious poetic justice in Cubillas' match-winning performance. He had been dismissed as well past his best by MacLeod and some of the Scots players, but while he was a veteran of the 1970 finals, he was still under 30 and at the peak of his powers.

ALLY MacLEOD

As if defeat was not bad enough, disgrace was to follow and winger Willie Johnston, one of the stars in the run up to the finals, was sent home when it emerged he had failed a mandatory drugs test at the end of the game. That made Johnston, who insisted he innocently took a hay fever cure, the only Scot on the planet with reason to be thankful for the result–had Scotland won FIFA could have reversed the score as a punishment for his crime.

Things, it seemed, could not get any worse, but they could and quickly did. On June 7, in Cordoba, the formality of beating Iran should have been completed. It wasn't and what developed was a hugely embarrassing 90 minutes that saw an own goal required for Scotland to scrape a 1-1 draw. Famously, after the match fans who had forked out a small fortune to get to South America gathered to barrack the players and officials with chants of "We want our money back...". It was hard to blame them.

Stories that some players who had not been picked were drinking in bars instead of being at the games did not help matters and back home the failures against Peru and Iran saw Ally MacLeod and his team come to be regarded somewhere between a joke and a national disgrace. As they moved towards the final group game against Holland, what had been billed as a dream about to become true had turned into a humiliating nightmare. In their opening group games – 3-0 against Iran and 0-0 with Peru – the Dutch had not quite produced the total football of 1974, but still looked a useful outfit and one that would surely demolish this sorry team.

For the first time in the competition Scotland were underdogs and with the introduction of the likes of Graeme Souness, had a more solid look. So, having twice been on the wrong end of shocks, the team proceeded to create one, winning 3-2 thanks to an excellent performance. It included a solo effort from Archie Gemmill that's gone down as being one of the best goals in World Cup history. For a brief spell it even looked as if the three-goal winning margin needed to secure qualification was achievable, but the stylish Dutch always had enough quality to stay in touch and did enough to get through to the second stage and then another losing appearance in the final.

ARCHIE GEMMELL

DIFFERENT APPROACH, SAME OUTCOME

Qualification for finals had come to be regarded as routine by the time Scotland, now managed by the legendary Jock Stein, made it through to Spain in 1982. The nation had learned from the experience of Argentina but Stein did not have to. Arguably the finest manager the country has ever produced, he was never guilty of making promises he could not keep. All he pledged was that everyone would give of their best and they did. For a third finals in a row, however, all that was to earn was the agony of being eliminated on goal difference.

Like eight years earlier in West Germany, things started well enough. Again meeting the smallest team first–this time it was New Zealand–an opening blitz saw Kenny Dalglish and John Wark (2), put Scotland well on top by half-time. Perhaps it was complacency, perhaps it was the heat but early second-half lapses allowed New Zealand to pull two goals back and although Steve Archibald and John Robertson netted at the other ended to help record a convincing win, those blemishes in the 'against' column were to prove costly.

So too were the four goals conceded to Brazil in the second group game, although few teams could resist the potent attacking play of Tele Santana's team, later to be dubbed, along with the Hungarians of 1954, as the best side to fail to win the trophy. In a one-sided match, Scotland still managed a moment of glory when Dundee United's Dave Narey struck the best goal of his illustrious career in the 18th minute.

There was no disgrace in that defeat in Seville but it meant that when the team returned to Malaga, the scene of the opening match, only a victory over the USSR would win a place in the second stage. Again, the match started well and Joe Jordan grabbed the opener on the quarter-hour mark. The Soviets, however, were a fine team and equalised after an hour. Then, as only Scotland can, the self-destruct button was pressed. Alan Hansen and Willie Miller, both fine defenders, moved to make what looked an easy clearance, but collided and allowed Ramaz Shenaglia to score. Only six minutes were left and while Graeme Souness levelled the scores three minutes later, it was too late and the team was heading home early yet again.

JOCK STEIN

SCOTLAND v NEW ZEALAND 1982 WORLD CUP

SCOTTISH TEAM v URUGUAY 1986 WORLD CUP

31

STEVE NICHOL v URUGUAY 1986 WORLD CUP

WITHOUT STEIN, ANOTHER FAILURE

The ultimate price was paid for a place in the Mexico finals of 1986. At Ninian Park in Cardiff in September 1985 a game of high drama became a night of huge tragedy when revered manager Jock Stein collapsed in the dugout near the end of the 1-1 draw that would see the team all but through. It was a heart attack and despite emergency treatment at the stadium, the most respected manager Scottish football had seen died. No one celebrated this qualification and even as the team, with Alex Ferguson now at the helm, took the field for the opening game against Denmark eight months later, a feeling of great loss remained.

This time the draw had done Scotland no favours and a group including Uruguay and two-time champions West Germany as well as the Danes, always looked like too tough. However a change in the set up of the finals–after the opening groups it would be straight knock out–meant third place could be good enough to get through. An opening 1-0 defeat against the Danes followed by a 2-0 reversal against the Germans made that seem unlikely but the way things worked out in other groups meant a win against the Uruguayans could see Scotland reach the second stage at last.

Again though it was not to be and on an afternoon that did nothing to enhance football's reputation as a great spectator sport (the South Americans were negative and ruthless in their pursuit of qualification) the game finished goalless.

GORDON STRACHAN SCOTLAND v DENMARK 1986 WORLD CUP

ANOTHER FINALS ANOTHER EXIT

Italia 90, regarded by some as the poorest finals ever, saw Scotland qualify for the fifth time on the trot and fail to get through the opening stage for the fifth time on the trot.

They even managed an Argentina-style disaster in losing the opening game to little-known Costa Rica. Like Peru and Iran in '78, the Costa Ricans were given no chance of causing an upset, though this time it was the media and support who were guilty of writing off the opposition and not the management. To be fair to the team as well, while the players could hardly argue they had performed well, on another day the chances created would surely have been enough to secure a victory. On top of that the Costa Ricans were not a bad side, something that was demonstrated when they went on to beat Sweden 2-1 in their final group game to secure a place in the second stage.

At least there was an immediate response to the embarrassment and Andy Roxburgh's team turned in a brave performance to beat much-fancied Swedes 2-1 in the second game thanks to goals from Stuart McCall and Mo Johnston. That night in Genoa was to be a memorable occasion both on and off the park. On it the team turned in a gutsy performance to earn the win. Off it the fans of both countries showed the world how to enjoy a sporting event, marching from the city centre to the stadium before kick off and enjoying a huge after-match party later in the evening.

The result meant a draw against now familiar World Cup rivals Brazil, would be enough to at last reach that second stage. In a tense game in Turin, things looked good for a long time but a late goal from Brazilian striker Muller broke Scottish hearts and sent the team home. Their opening game apart, Scotland had played reasonably well but yet again the effort was to be in vain.

JACKIE McNAMARA OF SCOTLAND v NORWAY 1998 WORLD CUP

MAURICE JOHNSTON v BRAZIL 1990 WORLD CUP

ANDY ROXBURGH

AFTER A GAP, MAIR O' THE SAME

Having led the team since 1986, steering them to a first-ever European Championship finals in Sweden in 1992 as well as Italia '90, national coach Andy Roxburgh decided to step down following failure to make the razzmatazz 1994 finals in the USA. That had brought to an end a remarkable sequence of five finals in a row but Roxburgh's successor, his assistant Craig Brown, immediately set about making sure normal qualification service would be resumed.

He led the team to Euro '96 in England, where only inferior goal difference again saw the team fail to reach the second stage of a major event, and then comfortably back to the World Cup.

France '98 would see Scotland get the honour of meeting defending champions Brazil in the opening game of the tournament and despite a 2-1 defeat, it was to prove a truly memorable occasion and one where defeat came only through a cruel own goal off defender Tom Boyd. The next match paired Brown's team with Norway and while Craig Burley's equaliser lifted spirits, there was a realisation that a great chance to earn victory had been squandered.

In a situation that had become so familiar over World Cup years, Scotland now had to win their final game, against Morocco, to get to the second stage. Not much was known about the North Africans, who had looked good in an opening draw with Norway but overawed by Brazil in their second game. Shortly after the game got underway, though, it was apparent they were the sharper, more talented, team and Brown's qualification dreams were shattered by a 3-0 defeat.

So, once again, a World Cup finals was to end in disappointment for Scotland, though given the limited resources of this squad, perhaps the big achievement this time was even getting to France.

And, despite eight unsuccessful finals appearances so far, there's always next time.....

The Scottish international side may never have threatened to win one of the game's major trophies but that lack of success should not be equated to a lack of talent. Down the years a steady stream of players of genuine world class have worn the dark blue with great distinction.

CRAIG BROWN

CRAIG BURLEY SCORES V NORWAY, FRANCE 1998

COLIN HENDRY & KEVIN GALLACHER FRANCE 1990

SCOTLAND FANS v BRAZIL, FRANCE 1998

BRAZIL'S ALDAIR CHALLENGES KEVIN GALLACHER FRANCE 1998

CHAPTER FOUR

European Championships

While, if only in terms of qualification, Scotland has enjoyed a long and relatively successful association with the World Cup, it was not until the 1990s that the international team enjoyed even modest success in the European Championships.

It took time for the competition, first won by the USSR in 1960 when it was known as the European Nations' Cup, to be regarded as important and even though it has now achieved the status of a major event, it still takes second place to the World Cup in terms of prestige. For a long time, Scottish fans were definitely of that opinion and so long as the World Cup finals were reached, they seemed happy to forgive the regular failure to reach its later stages. Over the course of the past decade that has change and heroic failures by the team in the 1992 finals in Sweden and again in England four years later have given the fans a greater liking for it, so much so that the struggles to reach Euro 2000 in Belgium and Holland did not go down well with the Tartan Army.

Of course, whatever its status, the European Championship finals arguably provide an even stiffer test than the World Cup when it comes to reaching the second round. On this narrower stage there are no minnows, though given the banana skin tendencies of Scottish teams against countries like Iran and Costa Rica that has not, perhaps, been a bad thing. Certainly, the quality of opposition on those first visit to the finals in '92 ensured that although the first hurdle of a major finals was again to prove too difficult a hurdle to overcome, the effort of Andy Roxburgh's team won wide praise.

Having battled through a difficult qualifying group that had included Romania, Bulgaria, Switzerland (a fight back against them to earn a draw from two goals down in Berne was probably the pivotal result of the series) and tiny San Marino, the draw then threw up even tougher tasks in the shape of joint favourites the Netherlands and Germany as well as the unpredictable talent of the former USSR states who would arrive in Scandinavia under the banner CIS. First up were the Dutch, the defending champions, who still boasted stars like Ruud Gullit, Frank Rijkaard and, the new kid on the block, Dennis Bergkamp. Despite that, Scotland held on for a long period before being cruelly sunk by a Bergkamp strike late on. Despite another brave performance, a 2-0 defeat against the Germans followed which meant qualification was no longer a possibility. Even so, the Swedish public had come to respect the team's battling approach and had fallen in love with the good natured fans and there was general delight as the Scots bowed out of the competition with a fine 3-0 win over the CIS.

Four years on, and after another difficult qualifying group, the draw every Scottish fan wanted saw the team, by now under the guidance of Craig Brown, paired with hosts England in Euro 96. The coach and his squad never lost sight of the importance of the other two fixtures against Holland and Switzerland, however, and as usual preparations for the whole event were thorough. They looked to be paying dividends as, with goalkeeper Andy Goram an inspiration, the team survived a Dutch siege to come away from the opening match with a goalless draw.

It was on to Wembley then in good spirits and for a long, long time on a blistering hot June afternoon it looked like that feeling of optimism was justified. Scotland enjoyed the better of a quiet first half and even the blow of losing a goal to the in-form Alan Shearer early in the second period, could not completely dampen spirits as Brown's team continued to play well. The difference between success and failure at this level, though, can be slim and a few explosive moments late in the game would see Scotland leaving the capital a beaten side. A fine effort from the entire team looked set to bear fruit when a period of pressure brought a penalty. Skipper Gary McAllister, a man who had served his country so well, stepped up to take the kick, but English goalkeeper David Seamen guessed right and blocked his disappointing shot. The opportunity to draw level, and possibly even go on and beat a flagging English team, had been squandered. The agony of that was compounded within moments when a breathtaking individual goal from Paul Gascoigne put the game beyond Scotland, who were left to consider what might have been.

All was not lost and victory in the final game against the Swiss, combined with a good English win over the Dutch, would still see them through. That equation would only lead to an agonising finale reminiscent of the World Cup failure in West Germany 22 years earlier. This time, though, the team did all they could and with the English racing into a four goal lead over the Dutch, a spectacular Ally McCoist goal looked like breaking that long major finals qualification duck. The second round appeared to beckon but cruelly for the Scots, and vitally for the underachieving Dutch, a late Patrick Kluivert goal at Wembley swung the goal difference balance in their favour and left Brown and his Tartan Army facing no more than a journey back north.

So, just like World Cups, Scotland still awaits progression to the knock out stages of the European Championships but those flirtations with the finals of Sweden and England have ensured that the event has now taken on considerable importance with the fans. Of course, that only adds to the pressure on the manager and players.

CHAPTER FIVE
Greats

As with all matters football, every fan will have their own opinion concerning who the very best were and, at the drop of a hat, be able to produce his or her own list of greats. What follows, therefore, is not claimed to be a definitive list of the very best to have represented the nation's team – just some of them.

KENNY DALGLISH (1971-1986).

The only Scot, so far, to break the 100 cap barrier and without argument the best of his generation. Throughout his career, however, Dalglish had to live with being tagged a better player for Celtic and then Liverpool, with whom he won three European Cups, than for his country. In the early years of an international career that stretched from the early seventies to mid-eighties and saw him accumulate a total of 102 appearances, that was probably a fair criticism, however. As time passed, and his cap count grew and as he matured into one of the finest performers in Europe, it became less appropriate. So good was 'King Kenny' that even when he could not quite put in the same quality of work as he did at club level, he still showed more than enough to justify his selection.

What Dalglish offered any of his team can be summed up with just one word–quality. He was not the biggest and certainly not the fastest, but he did have superb control, could pass and shoot with either foot and read the game like few Scots before or since. His vision meant he would often be yards ahead of the fastest defender, simply because he had summed up the situation quicker. For a player who supposedly was never quite at his best in internationals, his record equalling 30 goals was not a bad haul, particularly as he would often drop into deeper positions to act as provider rather than target man. On top of that the quality of his strikes was often superb and many international managers would have happily accepted his level of below par performance in every game.

KENNY DALGLISH

DENNIS LAW (1958-1974)

The Lawman, as he was and is known by Scots and followers of his beloved Manchester United, can lay claim to be among the most naturally gifted forwards this country has seen. He stands on the 30 international goals mark alongside Dalglish, the difference being his were scored in only a little over half the number of appearances the Celtic and Liverpool man made. In all Law won 55 caps during a career that saw him become one of the most feared strikers in Europe and which reached its peak as a member of the outstanding Manchester United side of the mid to late 1960s, though injury saw him miss their European Cup glory of 1968. During that period his apparent arrogance won him few friends among opposing fans, but his ability was always there for all to admire.

Born in Aberdeen in 1940, he made his international debut at just 18, scoring against Wales during a 3-0 win at Ninian Park, Cardiff. If ever a player deserved the chance to show his skills on the biggest stage–the World Cup Finals–it was Law, but he had to wait a long time for just one brief chance. It came in the 1974 finals in West Germany, by which time he was 34, had a troublesome knee problem and was in the final few weeks of his career. It was, perhaps, sentiment more than sound judgement that persuaded manager Willie Ormond to select him for the 2-0 win over Zaire in Dortmund and that was to be his last cap. Few, though, could be critical of the manager's decision to repay Law for the tremendous job he'd done for his country over 16 years and even at 34 and struggling for fitness, he was a threat to any defence. Manchester United had found that out when, as a Manchester City player, he had scored the goal that relegated them just a few weeks before the finals.

DENNIS LAW

BILLY BREMNER (1965-1976)

Not the greatest player to be capped by his country, though he possessed more skill than many people gave him credit for. A truly inspirational skipper for Scotland and the club he led to glory in England, Leeds United, he was small, but had the heart of a Lion. That mean both club and country were always assured of 100% commitment when Billy Bremner pulled on a jersey. He had an all action style and never-say-die attitude that was extremely effective when it came to getting the best out of those around him. The highlights of his distinguished international career included the famous win over then world champions England at Wembley in 1967 and leading the team in the West Germany World Cup finals in 1974. His finest moment there was his tenacious performance against Brazil, his 50th appearance, that helped earn a draw with the defending champions.

A year later and just one game short of equalling Dennis Law's record 55 caps, Bremner's international career came to an abrupt end after he stepped out of line during a trip to Denmark. That misdemeanour did nothing to diminish his immense popularity with the fans and quite rightly so. Sadly Bremner, a man who seemed as if he could run forever on the park, died of a heart attack at the age of just 54 in 1997.

BILLY BREMNER

DAVE MACKAY (1957-1964)

Like Bremner, Mackay has gone down in history as one of Scottish football's hard men. Also like Bremner, the Hearts, Spurs, Derby and Swindon man, who also led Derby to an English championship as their manager, was a talented and influential midfielder. At Hearts in the 1950s he was the inspiration of the most successful side in the club's history and at Spurs played a major role in the historic league and cup double of 1961.

For his country he was also a major player but two broken legs restricted him to just 22 appearances. Unfortunately for a man who hated losing, he was unlucky enough for one of them to be Scotland's humiliating 9-3 defeat by the English at Wembley in 1961. Like most of his team-mates, he was broken hearted after that game, though the 2-1 win on his return there two years later would rank as one of the highlights of his international career.

HUGHIE GALLACHER (1924-1935)

A controversial but immensely gifted centre-forward who was one of the game's first superstars. On the park he was a genius, scoring a total of 369 goals in an eight-club, 18 year senior career. Off it, he courted trouble and tragedy, landed on the wrong side of the law several times, was declared bankrupt at one point and eventually committed suicide by jumping in front of a train in 1957 when he was still only 54.

That was a dreadful and sad end for one of the great talents of any era and those who saw him play never forgot it. Gallacher, who was only a little over five feet tall, was one of the famous Wembley Wizards who conquered the English by 5-1 in their own backyard in 1928.

At that time he was at the very height of his powers and when he was in the mood few defences could cope. Despite his long career he won just 20 caps, but scored a remarkable 24 goals in the process. All but two of them came in the Home International Championship, making him the record scorer in the 101 years of the event.

ALAN MORTON (1920-1932)

A Wembley team-mate of Gallacher's in 1928, "the wee blue devil" has come to be regarded as one of the finest left wingers Scotland has produced, though he was in fact right-footed. Over 12 years from 1920–the year he moved from Queen's Park to Rangers–he won 31 caps, scored five goals and provided many more for players like Gallacher and another Wembley Wizard, Alex Jackson. He also made a record 11 appearances in the Scotland-England game. Despite his huge success, throughout his career he remained a part-timer, his duties as an engineer often meaning he would be at work on Saturday mornings before knocking off at lunch-time to play in big games for Rangers or Scotland.

ALEX JAMES (1926-1933)

The third member of the Wembley Wizards to appear in this chapter, Alex James was as big a star between the wars as any of that team and in the years to follow that famous 1928 victory, would become recognised as the man who made the great Arsenal team of the thirties tick. Although he moved to Highbury not long before his 28th birthday in 1929, he would spend eight glorious years as a player there and pick up four league championship medals as well as twice finishing on the winning side in FA Cup finals.

The tricky inside left's senior career had started at Raith Rovers in the early 1920s and his performances for the Kirkcaldy team soon had scouts from English teams heading for Stark's Park and Preston North End won the race for his signature in 1925. As he had done at Raith and would do at Arsenal, James became the linchpin of the team and during his twelve years south of the border, he came to be regarded as one of the most influential players in the First Division.

Despite this glittering record at club level he failed to gain the international recognition his skill deserved and over eight years from 1925, he would make just eight appearances for his country. Perhaps also a little unfairly, the history books often remember James more for his exceptionally baggy shorts than his prodigious talent.

JIMMY JOHNSTONE (1964-1974)

If it was a Ranger, Morton, who thrilled the country with wonderful wing play in the twenties and early thirties, it was a man from the other half of the Old Firm who would fulfil that role 40 years later.

In an era when the number of internationals taking place season by season was on the increase, it is somewhat hard to believe Jimmy Johnstone amassed just 23 caps between his debut in 1964 and his final appearance ten years later. When "Jinky" did play he was more than a handful for the very best defenders as he jinked his way up the right touchline, turning opponents inside out before delivering telling balls into the middle.

A likeable character and still a favourite with fans of Celtic, Johnstone was a genius on the field, but at times found himself in trouble off it, most notably while on duty with the Scotland squad in 1974 when he was cast adrift in a row boat at Largs and had to be rescued by the coastguard.

JIMMY JOHNSTONE

BILLY STEEL (1947-1953)

Many of those who regularly watched, or played against, Billy Steel believed he was one of the best footballers ever. Therefore, that he was one of the greatest talents in the history of the Scottish game, there can be little doubt.

Like Hughie Gallacher before him and Jim Baxter after, he was, however, a rebel whose lifestyle off the park often did little to help his performances on it. Even so he was still able to consistently thrill crowds at St Mirren, Morton, Derby County and Dundee – where he inspired the team to two League Cups – and also picked up 30 Scotland caps. In the process, he would score twelve goals and create many more, making him a huge favourite with the fans. Managers liked Steel too and his transfer from Cappielow to the Baseball Ground in 1947 was for a previously unequalled £15,000–breaking the British record, in fact, by over £5000. Three years later, Dundee's owner/manager paid a Scottish record of over £17,000 to bring him back north of the border. At that time his standing was such that he was in a position to negotiate a deal whereby he would spend most of the week in the west coast–he trained with Clyde – and only travel through to Dens Park to complete his match preparations the day before games.

When just 31, Steel decided to seek pastures new and emigrated to America where he continued to play football for a few more seasons, then worked in journalism in Los Angeles until his death in 1982.

JIM BAXTER (1961-1968)

Slim Jim, as he was affectionately known, kept the Scottish tradition of producing great entertainers going through the 1960s. On the park the Fifer, who made his name with Rangers, was a genius. Off it, he was a free spirit who enjoyed the swinging sixties to the full and that would cut short his career at the highest level. In later years it would even leave him fighting for his life.

After leaving Raith Rovers for Rangers in 1960, Baxter made his international debut in a 5-2 Hampden victory over Northern Ireland. He would soon become the darling of the fans for both club and country and is remembered for stealing the show in the Wembley victories of 1963 and, most famously of all, 1967.

In the '63 game, he got two of his three international goals, a disappointing total given his 34 appearances. Baxter's strength, though, was not in his goal scoring but his creative genius and he was a fantastic showman to boot.

In 1963, after his double had won the game for Scotland, he hid the match ball inside his jersey as he left the field in triumph. Although the SFA later demanded he return it, all they got for their trouble was an old ball, because nothing was going to make Baxter part with the real thing. Four years later and back at the same arena he was at his cheeky best as he helped inspire the Scots to a 3-2 win over the world champions.

Like so many great players, he also possessed a self-destruct button and his lifestyle caught up with him before the decade was out. He had moved from Rangers to Sunderland in 1965 and then on to Nottingham Forest. As his performances dipped, he would be freed from the City Ground and although he returned to Ibrox for a second spell, his playing days were over by the time he was 30 when he gave up the game to run a pub.

JIM BAXTER

DANNY McGRAIN (1973-1982)

A team mate of Johnstone's, McGrain was a fullback ahead of his time. At his peak he was one of his country's best and most consistent performers, and throughout his career was a credit to his profession. His nine years of service with the international team brought him 62 caps and appearances in two World Cup finals—it would have been three but for a leg injury that ruled him out of the calamitous 1978 event in Argentina.

In achieving all that McGrain had to triumph over adversity. He suffered a fractured skull in the early 1970s but fought back to fitness and even the discovery he was a diabetic could not halt his progress. Determination had a lot to do with his success but so too did skill and vision. He was helped too by the great Jock Stein's decision to switch him from his early midfield role to fullback. After moving to the rearguard, he never looked back and although he remained a defender for the rest of his highly successful career, McGrain was always a danger going forward.

DANNY McGRAIN

GEORGE YOUNG (1947-1957)

In the history of the national team there have been many great captains–a few are mentioned in this chapter–but few can put up as strong a case for title of the most influential of them all as the great George Young.

The first Scot to earn 50 caps–he won 53 in all–he led the team out on a record 48 occasions. His physical stature alone made him a natural choice for skipper but despite standing at 6 ft 2 ins and weighing in at around 15 stone in his prime, Young is rightly remembered for his skill, as well as for being hard, but fair, in the tackle. Sadly this superb player and ambassador for his sport was twice denied the opportunity to lead the country in the finals of the World Cup. In 1954 he was required for a close-season tour by Rangers, so did not go to Switzerland, while a harsh decision to drop him in the run up to the 1958 event in Sweden again saw him miss out. A gentleman off the park too, Young did not make a fuss, but instead accepted the selectors' right to choose what they felt was the best team and retired gracefully.

GEORGE YOUNG

GRAEME SOUNESS (1975-1986)

Gentleman footballer is probably not a phrase ever used to described Souness, though he always brought style to a football field. The midfielder, however, was as tough as he was talented and that meant he was extremely hard. His at times over zealous tackling meant he had his critics but no-one could deny his ability to perform at the very highest level. On occasion during his international career the Scots team would be found wanting, but however high the quality of opposition, Souness excelled. From his role in central midfield he was very often the perfect provider for the striking ability of Kenny Dalglish and their partnership at club level for Liverpool was instrumental in the Anfield club's European Cup successes of 1978, 1981 and 1984. Given his powerful shooting from outside the penalty area, it is surprising he scored just four times in his 54 appearances, though one quality strike did come in the '82 World Cup finals against the USSR.

Infamously he is remembered for a late tackle on Siggi Jonsson of Iceland in a qualifier in Reykjavik in May 1985 that shattered the wonder kid's knee and threatened to end a promising career.

Over a decade later, I interviewed Jonsson during his spell with Dundee United and asked for his thoughts about Souness.

"I do not bear him a grudge and that tackle led to me meeting Rod Stewart because I was stuck in the bar of the team hotel later that night with my knee heavily bandaged and Stewart came in. He recognised me and bought me a drink and had a chat about the game. I've never met either of them again, but if I do meet one of them, I know which one I'd prefer it to be!"

A bizarre reply, but quite a number of players who did battle with Souness over the years would share those sentiments.

GRAEME SOUNESS

JIMMY BROWNLIE (1909-1914)

If there is one position in which Scotland has never enjoyed a luxury of riches, it must surely be in goal. As a rule international managers, and before them selectors, have seldom had more than a couple of reasonable contenders to choose from at any given time. Even so, some fantastic 'keepers have represented their country and while his name is now barely even a distant memory in the team's history, Jimmy Brownlie goes down as one of the very best.

Like Alan Morton, Brownlie was never a full-time professional. A bricklayer to trade, this giant of a man still found time to develop into an exceptional player and in his sixteen appearances for Scotland, conceded a miserly eleven goals. At club level he played with Third Lanark for seventeen years and after retiring from playing, moved to Dundee United where he gave long service as secretary-manager.

BILL BROWN

BILL BROWN (1958-1966)

Fantastically agile, Bill Brown played second fiddle to the popular Tommy Younger on no fewer than 24 occasions during the 1950s before controversially being preferred to the skipper against France for the final match of the 1958 World Cup in Sweden. After that first cap he went on to make another 27 appearances, a record until Alan Rough emerged on the scene in the 1970s. A more flamboyant goalkeeper than the likes of Brownlie before him or Rough and Jim Leighton after, Brown was, nevertheless, a top class performer, enjoying a successful senior career with Dundee north of the border and Spurs down south, including their League and Cup double in 1961.

CHAPTER SIX

Managers

For the first 82 years of international football, the Scottish Football Association believed it could get along fine without needing to engage the services of a team manager. Since 1954, however, the association has made up for lost time, giving 13 different men the job on 15 occasions. Some have lasted longer than others, some have fared well, others not so well. All have had their eyes opened to the hazardous world that is international football.

The first national team boss was Andy Beattie, who was appointed for the World Cup in 1954. As is documented elsewhere in this book, Beattie's first spell in charge was brief, unsuccessful and, at times, unhappy. In his defence, as he was not given responsibility for picking the team he can hardly shoulder all the blame for a disappointing appearance in the finals. A part-time appointment, Beattie remained at the helm of Huddersfield Town, whom he guided to promotion to the English First Division. After becoming disenchanted with the Scotland set up, he announced his resignation during the World Cup in Switzerland and concentrated on keeping the Yorkshire club in the top flight.

After the experiment with Beattie, the SFA decided the services of a manager were an unnecessary luxury and for the best part of four years, until the next World Cup was on the horizon, soldiered on without one. When it was decided, with the finals in Sweden in mind, to make a new appointment, the choice of Manchester United's Matt Busby was a sound one. Of course, the Munich air disaster was to rob him of the chance to lead the team in the finals. Although he did resume his part-time duties again for a brief period later in 1958, Busby quickly decided he could not combine Scotland and Manchester United and decided to concentrate on his club career.

Early in 1959, the SFA returned to Beattie and offered him another chance to take the post. Given his dislike for the process of team selection by committee when he had first held the post, it seems a touch surprising that, with this system still in operation, he agreed to a second spell. He did and this time his tenure lasted longer. The position remained a part-time post and as his "day job" was now just across the border with Carlisle, carrying out his duties was easier. With the arrival of the swinging sixties, at club level Beattie was on the move again, heading considerably further south to Nottingham Forest. That made his dual role difficult and in October 1960 he requested permission to resign from his Scotland duties.

In their search for a replacement the SFA broke with conventional logic and appointed a man without a proven track record at club level. He was Ian McColl, who only a few months earlier had been turning out as player for Rangers in the Scottish Cup Final and who was still registered with the Ibrox club when he stepped into the job. McColl did not lack international experience, having won 14 caps in the fifties, but was completely untried as a manager. That did not prevent him leading Scotland to victory in over half his matches, though he has the misfortune to be remembered as the manager who led the team to Wembley in 1961 for a horrific 9-3 defeat. What is forgotten is that in the aftermath of that national disaster, McColl came within a whisker of securing qualification for the World Cup the following year, missing out only after a play-off defeat by Czechoslovakia in Brussels. It is worth remembering that the Czech team would go all the way to the final in Chile before losing to Brazil. Two years after the Wembley humiliation McColl had the satisfaction of a revenge win back there, thanks to two goals from "Slim Jim" Baxter, who he had handed his first cap shortly after becoming boss. In May 1963, just a month after that win, there was another dark day for the young manager as what was supposed to be a friendly against Austria at Hampden had to be abandoned eleven minutes from the end. With Scotland winning 4-1 the referee led the teams from the field following a string of flare ups, most of the blame for which was levelled at the Austrians, two of whom were sent off.

McColl, a man who shied away from the media spotlight, played a major role in moving responsibility for team selection towards the manager and away from the committees at SFA headquarters in Park Gardens. His rein came to an end in May 1965 and this time the SFA would move to the other end of the managerial spectrum when it came to the appointment of his successor. They opted not for a rookie but for one of the very best and most experienced men around in Celtic's Jock Stein. Later to serve the national team with great distinction, Stein's first spell in charge was short and unsuccessful. His brief was to get the team to the World Cup Finals in England in 1966 and when he failed to do that, like Beattie and Busby had done before him, he stood down to concentrate on his club job. In his case that was making Celtic into the most successful Scottish side ever.

The year most Scots football fans would like to forget – 1966 – dawned with the national team managerless and ended in a similar fashion. In between New Year's Day and Hogmany, there were two incumbents: John Prentice and Malcolm MacDonald. It was perhaps the rapid departure and arrival of another two part-time managers that finally persuaded the SFA that the Scotland job was now big enough for one man to be allowed to devote all his working hours to.

SCOTLAND MANAGER McCOLL

Bobby Brown, the last amateur player to appear for his country, had caught the eye as manager of St Johnstone and when approached he agreed to leave Muirton Park behind. As full-time boss he was officially given responsibility for picking the team and when his first game ended in a thrilling 3-2 win over world champions England at Wembley in 1967, his judgement seemed pretty sound. More good results would follow and after three reasonably successful years the manager was awarded a new contract. He would not serve its full duration and a dreadful run of results that saw just two wins and only three goals scored in eleven games from April 1970, led to him being relieved of his duties the following year.

Next to be handed the task of leading the national team was manager-of-many-clubs, the flamboyant Tommy Docherty. Like so many other of his jobs in football, his time with Scotland would not last long. It was also successful, though, both for the team and his own career. He took the team for just 12 games but recorded seven wins and two draws, with only three defeats. By November 1972 his work had impressed Manchester United enough for them to swoop and offer him the chance to succeed Frank O'Farrell at Old Trafford. Taking that job would see his income soar and that, plus the lure of managing the biggest club side in Britain, proved too tempting to turn down. While there was some disenchantment over his leaving, Docherty could head south knowing he had done a good job.

With Docherty gone, the SFA went back to St Johnstone for their next manager and handed the task of getting Scotland back to the World Cup Finals to one of the game's quiet men. Shy and retiring, Willie Ormond was everything Docherty was not and in his early games, Scotland's results were everything Docherty's were not. While, however, Ormond took time to find his feet, once he did he went on to gain huge respect for the way in which he handled the job and would serve longer than any of his predecessors.

In doing that he survived a few shaky spells and had to recover from a nightmare start. His first game was the SFA Centenary match against England. It took place at Hampden on February 14, 1973 and turned out to be football's version of the St Valentine's Day massacre. Unfortunately it was Scotland who were to be the victims, losing 5-0 to an English side that demonstrated little respect for the romance of the occasion. Three months later the Home International Championship followed and Ormond's team struggled again. In Wrexham two goals from Arthur Graham against the Welsh earned a much needed morale boosting victory. However, it was quickly followed by defeats against Northern Ireland, 2-1 at Hampden, and England, at Wembley by a single goal. Matters did not improve much when the next two games also resulted in single goal defeats. While that was disappointing in Berne against Switzerland, when world champions Brazil visited Hampden at the end of June and only just managed to win, there were some signs of encouragement.

TOMMY DOCHERTY

Even so, by the time Czechoslovakia flew over to Hampden in September of that year, Ormond had two very good reasons for seeking a win. First off, it was a make-or-break World Cup qualifier and if Scotland won a place in West Germany the following summer would be in the bag. Second, if the game ended in defeat, the pressure for him to be sacked would be immense and probably irresistible. Cometh the hour, cometh the man and on one of the most dramatic Hampden nights ever, goals from Jim Holton and a young Joe Jordan saw the Scots come from behind to end a 16-year wait for another visit to the finals. In West Germany Ormond and his team were desperately unlucky not to progress to the second stage and when they returned home following elimination only on goal difference, it was to a hero's welcome. In the region of 10,000 supporters were waiting as their plane touched back down in Scotland. If just a few months before those finals Ormond's position has been in some doubt, he was now a popular figure and would come to be regarded as one of the most successful Scottish managers.

His standing was diminished somewhat by another heavy defeat at the hands of England, 5-1 at Wembley a year after the World Cup. He continued in the job for another two years before he accepted an offer from Hearts, arch-rivals of the Hibs team he had starred in during the 1950s, to become their manager. Before he left he had set the ball rolling on another successful World Cup qualifying campaign, although that was something his successor would live to regret.

As had often been the case when the Scotland manager's job was up for grabs, Jock Stein seemed the obvious choice to fill the vacancy and once Willie Ormond had packed his bags and headed for Tynecastle, there is little doubt the Celtic manager was the man wanted by the SFA. As had been the case before, they would be disappointed, for Stein preferred to continue his pursuit of even more trophies at Celtic Park. If the first choice was an obvious one, so too was the next in line and the search soon moved from the west to the north east and Aberdeen. The man now being sought after was the Dons fast-talking boss Ally MacLeod, who had just taken the League Cup to Pittodrie only a little over a year after moving up to the Granite City. Aberdeen had been attracted to him by the work he had put in at Ayr United and it was his successes at both clubs that persuaded the SFA he was the man to lead the national team.

If talk won matches, then MacLeod was a world champion and after qualifying for the 1978 finals in Argentina, he convinced the land that was what his team was about to become. What they managed was embarrassment and even a win over eventual finalists Holland in the closing group game could not disguise a poor performance in the tournament. Ally's famous army had now turned against him, perhaps a touch unfairly given they had allowed themselves to get as carried away as he had in the run up to Argentina. Still, he managed to hang on for one more game, against Austria, but when that ended in defeat, he resigned and returned to the club where, for him, it had all began – Ayr United.

That left the door open for another move for Jock Stein. By now his enormously successful Celtic career had ended and he had moved on to Leeds United. He had been at Elland Road only a matter of weeks, but when the chance to become national manager for a second time arose, he could not say no.

During his playing career, the former miner from Lanarkshire, was a wholehearted player but possessed no more than average ability. His senior career had started during the war at Albion Rovers, for whom he played part-time while continuing to work down the mines. In 1949, he ended seven years as a Rovers player when he moved to Wales to turn out for Llanelli. After two years there he returned home for his first spell with Celtic and while initially he was there to help with the reserves and youth team, he went on to become centre-half and skipper of the first team, winning the double in 1954. A year later injury forced him into coaching on a full-time basis and it was from then on he would really come into his own.

In 1960, Stein moved from Glasgow to Fife to become manager at Dunfermline, where he quickly led the Pars to a Scottish Cup triumph. Four successful years at East End Park saw him attract Hibs' attention but his stay at Easter Road was to be short-lived, for after less than a year in the capital he was given the task of restoring past glories at Celtic. Just as he had with Dunfermline, he quickly led the Bhoys to victory in the Scottish Cup and the following year saw the start of a run of nine titles in a row–in all he would win the title ten times. His greatest achievement as a manager came in Lisbon in 1967 when his talented side beat the might Internazionale of Milan to become the first British club to lift the European Cup.

Of course, nothing he did as Scotland manager could surpass that feat, but for the final seven years of his life Big Jock would lead his country with distinction and in the process add a professionalism to the national team set-up that had at times been lacking under previous regimes.

Like those before him, Stein failed to secure qualification for a European Championship finals, his unsuccessul attempts coming in1980 and 1984. With little fuss he led the team to the World Cup in Spain in '82. There, they failed to qualify for the second stage but were beaten only by a Brazilian side that was arguably the most talented in the competition that year. Three years later he was on the verge of doing the same again but on what should have been one of the great nights of his career, he would collapse and die of a heart attack.

The tragedy occurred at Ninian Park, Cardiff on September 10, as his team battled hard for a 1-1 draw that would all but secure passage to the Mexico finals in 1986. Watching from the dugout, Stein had seen the injury-hit Scots battle back from losing an early Mark Hughes goal to equalise late on via a Davie Cooper penalty. Ten minutes later the final whistle sounded and the fans headed off for their celebrations, knowing that a two-leg play off against minnows Australia was the only obstacle between their team and Mexico. As news from the stadium spread, however, the victory party was brought to an abrupt halt. Big Jock had taken ill in the dugout near the end of the game and died later in the treatment room at Ninian Park.

A country that had produced some of the finest managers ever had lost the greatest of them all. Suddenly getting to the World Cup did not seem so important any more.

Even so, the job Jock Stein had started and almost finished, had still to be completed. The man handed the task of doing that, was his number two, the highly successful Aberdeen boss Alex Ferguson. After one friendly against East Germany–it finished goalless–Fergie led the team into the Australian games and duly qualified for the finals, thanks to goals from Davie Cooper and Frank McAvennie at Hampden and a no-score draw in the return in Melbourne. He then guided the team through a mainly successful warm-up programme in the first half of 1986, when England were the only team to both score against and beat the Scots. In Mexico, however, things were different and Ferguson's team failed to win any of the three games against Denmark, West Germany and the cynical Uruguayans, in what was dubbed the group of death. Aware of that, it was felt Ferguson had done enough to be given the job permanently, but he preferred to concentrate on his club career at Aberdeen and then Manchester United, so a new boss had to be found.

The SFA's choice of successor raised a few eyebrows and in something of a throw back to the appointment of Ian McColl over a quarter of a century earlier, the job was given to a man with no managerial experience, Andy Roxburgh. One thing Roxburgh did know was coaching, having spent a decade at the SFA, latterly as the full-time director of coaching. In that time he had produced a string of successful youth teams and many of the players he had worked with as teenagers were emerging as full internationals by the time his duties were extended to take in responsibility for the big team. So, while handing Roxburgh the job was a gamble, it was not as big a risk as many people thought. The logic behind it was reasonable, after all over the years many good club managers had found giving up day-to-day involvement with players difficult, but that was never a problem for a man who was familiar with the national team set-up thanks to his long service at Park Gardens.

Once he became the main man, Roxburgh started by maintaining the tradition of failure in European Championship qualifiers, but performed with distinction in getting the team to the World Cup in 1990 despite being faced with a group including France, who had performed so valiantly in the finals of 1982 and 1986. During his four years in charge before Italy, he became known for

ALEX FERGUSON & JOCK STEIN

his meticulous planning, but no matter how well the team was prepared for a fifth finals in a row, it was still not good enough to make it past the opening stage. That was a disappointment for the manager, but he and his team had not let anyone down and two years later he chalked up a first when he became the first Scottish manager to guide the team to a European Championship Finals. They were held in Sweden and were to be the fairy tale finals, not for Scotland but for Denmark, who had not even qualified but were called in at the last minute when Yugoslavia were thrown out and went on to win the event. The Scots, while again exiting a major tournament without getting past the first round, did leave their mark. Brave performances could not make up for the gap in terms of quality to Holland and Germany, but the team bowed out with an exhilarating win over the CIS – most of the states that had previously made up the USSR and which continued to play under one banner for a brief period after its break-up. The fans were once again outstanding, backing the team superbly despite the opening defeats and earning praise from both the Swedish authorities and UEFA.

Given his limited resources, the event also did Roxburgh's growing reputation on the international scene no harm. It would even survive the failure to reach the World Cup in America in 1994. That was only fair and most pundits realised all good things must end and in qualifying for five consecutive tournaments from 1974 through to 1990, a small country had performed exceptionally well. In seven years in charge Roxburgh could look back and say he had done well too, but perhaps he felt he had done all he could. Once it was confirmed the team could not make the USA, he stood down, then joined FIFA, an organisation that held him in high regard and for whom he had undertaken "summer jobs" as an observer at events like the 1986 World Cup in Mexico and even the youth World Cup at home in Scotland three years later.

That the SFA gave Roxburgh's assistant Craig Brown the job, was no great surprise, though there was the usual speculation over who the new manager would be. Brown got the job on a temporary basis first and then, a few hours before a clash with Malta, was handed a long-term contract.

A former youth international whose progress as a player was curtailed by a series of knee operations that forced him to retire before his 30th birthday, Brown had served a long apprenticeship as assistant manager so while the usual list of big-name possibles was examined by the Press, it was always likely that the association would opt for the man who was already well known and trusted by them.

A former teacher like his close friend and predecessor, he also shared Roxburgh's distinction of never having managed a club at the highest level in Scotland. Brown was, however, a successful assistant to Willie McLean at Motherwell and gained a astute reputation as a manager in his own right at Clyde. He knew his way around the international scene as well and in addition to his duties with the top team, enjoyed success with teams right up to under-21 level.

In his first five years in the job he would emulate Roxburgh in leading Scotland to the finals of two major tournaments – Euro '96 and France '98. Given that he had what could best be described as an ordinary, if extremely dedicated, squad of players, achievement should not be underestimated. Of course, he was unable to break the trend of early exits from finals and, after France in particular, that led to some criticism, but in the cold light of day just getting to that stage was as much as anyone had a right to expect.

After those finals some believed Brown would step out of the limelight, but he expressed a desire to continue. Given the hard work he has put in and the relative success he has enjoyed with limited resources, it seems only right he has been allowed to carry on in this most testing of jobs.

CHAPTER SEVEN

Famous Matches

Sweet successes against the auld enemy

Scotland 7 England 2, Hampden, 1878

Even at a time when the Scottish team was the dominant force in the annual internationals with England and Wales, this was something spectacular. The English had not beaten the Scots since the second game of the series some six years earlier and accordingly went in as the underdogs. Very few, however, would have predicted a home victory by anything like this margin and until this day it remains the biggest Scottish win over the auld enemy.

This was also a prime example of why the men from the north won so many of the games before the turn of the century. While the English team stuck doggedly to old-style individualism, their hosts were intent on playing a passing game and those tactics were to work perfectly. From the kick off Scotland dominated and before too long it was obvious to an ecstatic home crowd that it was going to be a case of by how many rather than if. This most famous of the early victories also included the fixture's first hat-trick, scored by Vale of Leven's John McDougall.

Making what was to prove his fifth and last appearance against England was the talented goalkeeper Robert Gardner, not that he was required to show his abilities that afternoon. Gardner had been in goal for the historic first international in '72 and was widely regarded as the best 'keeper of the time, even though he had only moved from the outfield not long before that game. As well as a playing career at Queen's Park and then Clydesdale, he also served as president of the Scottish Football Association in 1887-88.

Teams:
Scotland: Gardner; McIntyre, Vallance, Campbell, Kennedy, Richmond, McGregor, McDougall, Highet, McKinnon, McNeill.
England: Walker; Lyttelton, Hunter, Bailey, Jarrett, Cursham, Fairclough, Wace, Wylie, Heron, Mosforth.

England 1 Scotland 5, Wembley, 1928

The team that was to become known as the Wembley Wizards and which recorded one of the most famous wins ever in England's backyard, was given only an outside chance of success in the build up to this second meeting of the countries at Wembley. With home advantage and the likes of Everton goal machine Dixie Dean in their line up, the English had every reason to believe it would be the visitors who would end up with the wooden spoon. Dean was a superb header of the ball, but aerial attack was hardly an option that was open to the Scots. To the disbelief of many the SFA selectors had chosen a forward line of Alec Jackson, Jimmy Dunn, Hughie Gallacher, Alex James and Alan Morton. Of that quintet only Jackson stood above 5 ft. 6in.

As well as over this lack of height up front, there was disquiet about the number of home-based Scots in the line-up. Only talented young goalkeeper Jack Harkness, at that time still an amateur with Queen's Park, Dunn (Hibs) and Morton (Rangers), played their club football north of the border.

On to the action, and with the game only a few minutes old, the prophets of doom were forgotten, though there was a scare when England hit a post in their first attack. It would be claimed later that the next time the home team touched the ball was to restart after going a goal down. Whether or not that was indeed the case, a definite fact is that the Scots shocked their confident opponents when, following a sweeping move started by skipper Jimmy McMullan, Jackson stole in from the right to head home a Morton cross.

For a time England pressed hard for the equaliser, but just before the break the goal that would allow Scotland to relax and turn on the style in the second half came. Alex James got it with a sweet shot from the edge of the penalty area and even with 45 minutes still to be played, the team seemed to sense victory was theirs.

In the second half, Jackson went on to get his hat-trick and James his own second. England did get a consolation goal through Bob Kelly, a Huddersfield team-mate of Jackson's, in the final minute, but nothing could disguise Scotland's total dominance. Gracious in victory, Scots skipper McMullan would later express his belief that the conditions had played a part in the winning margin. It had rained heavily overnight and prior to kick off. McMullan felt the sodden pitch gave the smaller Scots players the advantage and they made the most of it.

Teams.

England: Hufton; Goodall, Jones, Edwards, Wilson, Healless, Hulme, Kelly, Dean, Bradford, Smith.
Scotland: Harkness, Nelson, Law, Gibson, Bradshaw, McMullan, Jackson, Dunn, Gallacher, James, Morton.

England 2 Scotland 3, Wembley, 1967

If there is a Scottish victory at Wembley that vies with the 1928 win for importance, it has to be the stylish success of 1967. England, as many a beleaguered Scot was already tired of hearing, had won the World Cup at the home of football in 1966 and were unbeaten since. Scotland, who had not even qualified for the finals, would be given a lesson by Alf Ramsay's wingless wonders and were really only heading south to pay homage to the world's greatest side. Well, pride does come before a fall and the English were about to come crashing down from a very great height.

The score does not reflect just how comfortabe the win was and two England goals in the last five minutes had more to do with Scotland players relaxing when 2-0 up than any great fight back by the home team. This was a game the Scots took by the scruff of the neck from the early stages and perhaps the only surprises in the first half were that it took them 28 minutes to take the lead, through Dennis Law, and that they only led by a single goal come the interval. Scotland's cause was helped by an injury to towering home centre-half Jack Charlton. He was limping badly for most of the 90 minutes and was pushed out wide for the entire second half. In some quarters that was used as an excuse for defeat, but with nine other fit members of the World Cup winning side still on the park – Jimmy Greaves for Roger Hunt was the only change from the '66 line up – the English still represented a formidable force. Even so, Scotland had the better of the second half and looked home and dry when Celtic's Bobby Lennox got the second goal with just twelve minutes left.

The Scots were showboating now, a little too much in fact, and the brave Charlton, possibly the only Englishman to come out of the match with any credit, gave them a fright when he pulled one back in the 85th minute. The response to that was swift and two minutes later Jim McCalliog restored the two goal lead. There was still time for World Cup hero Geoff Hurst to again reduce the defecit, but by then victory was secure and the Scotland team heroes.

Incidentally, watching from the Press box that day in his capacity as football correspondent for The Sunday Post was Jack Harkness, one of the stars of the Wembley Wizards' victory 39 years earlier. He recorded his delight at the win and even forgave "old hands" Dennis Law and Jim Baxter, who sat on the ball at one point, for becoming too cocky in the closing minutes.

Teams:

England: Banks; Cohen, Wilson, Stiles, J. Charlton, Moore, Ball, Greaves, R. Charlton, Hurst, Peters.

Scotland: Simpson; Gemmell, McCreadie, Greig, McKinnon, Baxter, Wallace, Bremner, McCalliog, Law, Lennox.

On the World Cup trail

Scotland 3 Switzerland 2, Hampden Park, 1957

Having performed miserably at the 1954 finals, Scotland wanted to get back to the World Cup at the first time of asking and by the time the last qualifying game, against the Swiss, came round, they knew only a win would secure a place in Sweden the following summer.

The aim was simple, achieving it was to prove more difficult and it front of almost 59,000 fans, the Scots had to fight all the way. In a tough encounter Tommy Docherty, by then an established international, set up Archie Robertson for the opener just short of the half hour mark. Minutes later Docherty turned unintentional provider at the other end and his error allowed Riva to equalise for the visitors. Early in the second half Jackie Mudie restored the home lead and when an Alex Scott strike was allowed to stand despite strong, and probably justified, Swiss claims for offside, a place in the finals looked secure. In the 80th minute, though, Vonlanthen grabbed Switzerland's second goal and by the final whistle the home hero was not one of the Scottish scorers but 'keeper Tommy Younger who kept the opposition out with a string of fine saves.

Teams:
Scotland: Younger; Parker, Caldow, Fernie, Evans, Docherty, Scott, Collins, Mudie, Robertson, Ring.
Switzerland: Parlier: Kernen, Morf, Grobety, Koch, Schneiter, Chiesa, Ballaman, Meier, Vonlanthen, Riva.

Scotland 2 Czechoslovakia 1, Hampden 1973

One of the great Hampden occasions as Willie Ormond's team ended a 16 year wait for another successful World Cup qualifying campaign. Despite indifferent form following Ormond's appointment to replace Manchester-bound Tommy Docherty in the manager's job, 100,000 fans packed into the national stadium on a rainy September evening knowing a win over the skilful Czechs would book a place in West Germany the following summer.

As kick off approached the fans were optimistic, but it is hard to understand why. The previous four games had been lost and a team lacking in confidence had been able to muster just a single goal in that run. In an attempt to end the goal drought veteran Dennis Law was recalled to win his 50th cap. It was, however, two of the emerging generation of young Scots who would finish the night on the score sheet. Before they took centre stage there was to be an early scare as Celtic 'keeper Ally Hunter was beaten at his near post by a Nehoda shot to give the Czech's a shock lead.

Into the limelight stepped big Jim Holton, Manchester United's 22-year-old centre-half, to ease the nerves with a headed equaliser before the interval. Roared on by the partisan crowd, Scotland swept forward in the second half. Eventually the breakthrough came when Willie Morgan crossed for substitute Joe Jordan to head the winner. The Leeds United striker was just 21 and had made only a handful of appearances, but he had scored one of the most important goals of his life.

Teams:

Scotland: Hunter; Jardine, McGrain, Bremner, Holton, Connelly, Hay, Law, Morgan, Dalglish (Jordan), Hutchison.

Czechoslovakia: Viktor, Pivarnik, Samek, Zlocha, Bendl, Bicovsky, Adamec, Kuna, Nehoda, Stratil, Pananka.

Wales 0 Scotland 2, Anfield, 1977.

Ally MacLeod's reign as Scotland manager will forever be associated with the humiliation and scandal of the 1978 World Cup in Argentina, but it also had its high points, particularly in the manner in which the team qualified. Having already taken care of European champions Czechoslovakia, the Scots route to the Argentine was then blocked by Wales, who had still to be faced away from home. Such was the demand for tickets that the Welsh FA decided to switch the game to Liverpool's Anfield stadium, a move they must later have regretted. The capacity was set at a little over 50,000 and showing their usual endeavour when it comes to such matters, the Tartan Army managed to snap up in the region of 30,000 of them – far more than had been allocated by the Welsh. That meant that come the start of the match the atmosphere was more like Glasgow than Cardiff or Wrexham. It was hardly surprising, therefore, that the Scots grabbed the initiative early on. The Welsh team, though, contained quality performers like Terry Yorath, Joey Jones and Liverpool legend John Toshack and they gradually fought their way back into the game. As the game wore on it grew more and more tense until Scotland finally edged ahead just twelve minutes from time.

The lead came via a penalty award that would later be proved extremely harsh on the Welsh. Joe Jordan and David Jones leapt together for a Willie Johnstone throw in and although the ball struck a hand, it was impossible to tell whose. The wise move would have been to wave play on, but French referee Robert Wurtz decided Jones was the offender and pointed to the spot. Later, pictures showed the ball had struck Jordan, so at the time it was not surprising that the Welsh protested. The referee was unmoved, as was Don Masson, who calmly slotted the ball past 'keeper Dai Davies. Anfield erupted and victory celebrations began. But the excitement was not over. As Wales threw men forward in a desperate attempt to save the game, Scotland broke down the right, the ball was crossed and Kenny Dalglish marked his appearance on his club ground with a perfect header past the helpless Davies. Scotland were through, Liverpool was annexed for the night and MacLeod basked in the glory, little knowing what lay just around the corner.

Teams:

Wales: Davies, R Thomas, J Jones, Mahoney, D Jones, Phillips, Flynn, Sayer, Yorath, Toshack, M Thomas.

Scotland: Rough Jardine, Donachie, Masson, McQueen, Forsyth, Dalglish, Hartford, Jordan, Macari, Johnston.

PETER LORIMER v ENGLAND

SCOTLAND TEAM WALK THE PITCH BEFORE THE MATCH v BRAZIL, FRANCE 1998

SCOTLAND SALUTE THE FANS

WILLIE ORMOND CELEBRATES AFTER BEATING CZECHOSLOVAKIA, 1973.

HAPPY SCOTS v CZECHOSLOVAKIA, 1973.

JOHN COLLINS SCORES FROM THE PENALTY SPOT v BRAZIL, FRANCE 1998

CHRISTIAN DAILLY SHOOTS FOR GOAL v NORWAY, FRANCE 1998

GORDON STRACHAN IN ACTION v GERMANY

DAVE McPHERSON IN ACTION v SWEDEN, ITALY, 1990

GOUGH, MILLER & McLEISH CELEBRATE